SPORTS ZONE!

HUT! HUT! HIKE!

Written by
ANDREW MARANISS

Illustrated by
AISHWARYA TANDON

BRANCHES™
SCHOLASTIC INC.

Stay in the game by reading these SPORTS ZONE! books!

1

2

3

TABLE OF CONTENTS

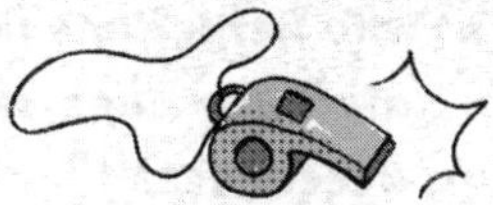

For Alison, Eliza, Charlie, and Kendall, in celebration of our "Joey Stories!" — AM

To my "teammates" who helped me in completing this book. And to Satvik for cheering for your "Aishwaya deeedeeee!!!" — AT

Library of Congress Cataloging-in-Publication Data

Names: Maraniss, Andrew, author. | Tandon, Aishwarya, illustrator.
Title: Hut! Hut! Hike! / Andrew Maraniss ; illustrated by Aishwarya Tandon.
Description: First edition. | New York : Branches/Scholastic, Inc., 2025. | Series: Sports Zone! ; 1 | Audience: Ages 6–8 | Audience: Grades 1–3 | Summary: Neighborhood friends Jasper, Mo, and Ruby learn about facing insecurities and also teamwork, competition, and love for sports when they try out for an organized flag football team and play their first real game. Includes football history, player biographies, and flag football rules. Identifiers: LCCN 2024016377 |
Subjects: LCSH: Flag football—Juvenile fiction. | Football for children—Juvenile fiction. | Football teams—Juvenile fiction. | Football stories. | CYAC: Flag football—Fiction. | Football—Fiction. | Football teams—Fiction. | LCGFT: Sports fiction. Classification: LCC PZ7.1.M36976 Hu 2025 | DDC [E] —dc23/eng/20240528 LC record available at https://lccn.loc.gov/2024016377

ISBN 978-93-5954-918-7

Printed in India at Shiv Shakti Printing and Trading Co., Haryana
This reprint edition, September 2025

Edited by Katie Carella
Book design by Jaime Lucero

CHAPTER 1

LIVING-ROOM FOOTBALL

The first thing nine-year-old Jasper McCoy learned about playing living-room football is that you need pillows. Lots and lots of pillows. And a beanbag chair, dog bed, Hula-Hoop, and fluffy blankets. Plus a football, of course—preferably a red squishy one.

You also need an announcer voice, the kind you hear on TV on Sunday afternoons. When Jasper is playing ball, he often hears this voice in his head: *And there's a pass from Jasper . . . to Jasper! He races around the beanbag chair, leaps over two pillows, and lands on the fluffy blankets for a touchdown! Jasper wins the Super Bowl!*

Every day when Jasper gets home from school, he has a favorite routine. He takes his dog, Kendall, for a walk around the block. He finishes his homework, practices the piano, and reads a book on the couch with his mom.

At around 5:30 p.m., he peeks outside, watching the driveway for his dad's car to pull up.

When his dad walks in the door, Jasper leaps up. "Ready to play football?!"

Sometimes Jasper's dad is tired. Sometimes he needs to mow the lawn or do something super important like set his fantasy football lineup. But he always says yes to playing ball with Jasper.

"You're on!" his dad replies, grabbing the football.

Jasper lines up beside his dad, ready to go out for a pass on a play that his dad named Steamboat Springs.

"Hut, hut, hike!" barks Mr. McCoy.

Jasper runs across the room, turns at the sofa, skips over the Hula-Hoop, and holds up his hands as he dashes by the bookcase.

Jasper's dad raises his right arm. Then he throws a perfect spiral five feet in front of Jasper's path.

Jasper dives across the blankets and soars through the air. He's headed toward the beanbag chair. But the throw is a bit too far, and Jasper can't get there in time.

Crash! A vase filled with flowers smashes to the floor. Water and broken glass fly everywhere.

"Jasper, you're never playing football in the house again!" his mom yells from down the hall.

His dad shrugs his shoulders. "She's probably right," he says.

"But it was *your* throw that broke the vase, Dad," Jasper replies.

"I think the point is that the living room isn't the best place to play football," his dad says. "You'll have to play outside from now on."

Jasper sighs in frustration. *And just like that, living-room football is over!* Jasper hears his announcer voice say. *The best player in history, Jasper McCoy, is forced to retire at age nine.*

"Is it okay if I go over to Mo's for dinner tonight?" Jasper asks as he helps his dad clean up the mess. Mo Garcia, a fellow third grader at Raintree Elementary, is Jasper's best friend.

"Sure thing, kiddo," his dad replies.

Jasper runs down the hall, through the screened-in porch out back, and over to the house next door. Mo will never believe what's just happened.

CHAPTER 2

BREAKFAST FOR DINNER

"Hi, Mr. and Mrs. Garcia," Jasper calls out as he bursts through his neighbors' kitchen door. "What's for dinner?"

Jasper comes over to the Garcias' house so much, it's like he's part of the family.

"Your favorite—breakfast for dinner!" Mr. Garcia says with a smile. "We have eggs, sausage, hash browns, and fruit."

"Sounds perfect," Jasper replies. "It's been the worst day ever. My mom and dad said I can't play football in the house anymore!"

"Your parents are smart," Mrs. Garcia says. "My little Mo will never play football *anywhere*. It's way too dangerous. All that tackling and grunting and groaning. It's a wonder someone doesn't get hurt on every single play."

Mo sighs. "First of all, I'm not little!" he says. "And second, nobody ever got hurt from grunting or groaning."

"Actually, your uncle David did," his dad replies, placing a pan into the oven. "Groaned so hard one Thanksgiving, he split his pants."

Jasper laughs, but Mo rolls his eyes and waves for Jasper to come up to his room.

They run upstairs and dive onto the floor, knocking over a stack of football cards.

Jasper scoops up the cards, sorting them into piles of offensive and defensive players.

OFFENSE AND DEFENSE

In a football game, the offense controls the ball, attempting to move down the field and score points. Players on defense try to stop them.

Offensive positions include:

QUARTERBACK

RUNNING BACK

WIDE RECEIVER

Defensive positions include:

LINEMAN

LINEBACKER

CORNERBACK

He places eleven football cards in front of him, one for every offensive position.

Then he pushes a card straight ahead, then over to the left, just like a wide receiver running a down-and-out.

He tosses the quarterback card toward the receiver. It lands right on top.

Pass complete! Jasper's announcer voice says in his head.

"So why can't you play football inside anymore?" Mo asks.

"My dad and I broke a vase tonight," Jasper admits.

"Maybe it's time to play on a real team on a real football field?" Mo suggests.

"I just don't know if I want to play kiddie ball with a bunch of nine-year-olds. Have you seen how many Super Bowls I've won at home?" says Jasper. "I might wait until middle school when I'll have some competition."

"Middle school? No way I'm waiting that long! Let's find a team we can play on together now," Mo says. "But how will I convince my mom to let me play?"

"Beats me," Jasper says. "There's only one person who might have an answer . . ."

"Ruby!" Jasper and Mo say at once.

Ruby Jones is Jasper and Mo's best friend who lives down the block. She has had the answer to every question the boys have had since kindergarten.

"Dinner's ready!" Mo's dad calls up from downstairs. "Come and get it!"

Once breakfast-for-dinner is over, it will be time to pay Ruby a visit.

CHAPTER 3

RUBY TO THE RESCUE

Jasper and Mo walk into Ruby's house and take off their shoes, like they have done a million times before.

"Hello, Jasper! Good evening, Mo," says Ruby's mom as the boys rush past her. "Ruby is upstairs reading."

"Hi, Dr. Jones!" Jasper and Mo yell as they run up to Ruby's room. Ruby's mom is a history professor at State University.

Ruby's walls are covered with pictures of her sports heroes, including posters of her favorite quarterbacks, Doug Williams and Patrick Mahomes.

DOUG WILLIAMS

In 1988, QB Doug Williams led Washington to victory in Super Bowl XXII, and he was named Super Bowl MVP. Doug was the first Black QB to start and win a Super Bowl, leading the way for other Black QBs in the NFL.

PATRICK MAHOMES

As a young quarterback, Patrick Mahomes took the NFL by storm. By the time he was just twenty-eight years old, he had already led Kansas City to three Super Bowl victories and won two MVP awards.

But Ruby is not just a football fan. Baseball, tennis, basketball: Ruby loves them all. And she knows a ton of sports history.

"Ruby," Mo says, "we have a question. A problem, really. We need your help."

"Uh-oh," Ruby replies. "Sounds like we need to take Kendall for a walk."

Whenever the boys have an important question for Ruby, the conversation always takes place at the dog park.

The three friends walk over to Jasper's house to get Kendall. Then they go to Miss Daisy's Bark Park, a tree-lined stretch of grass surrounded by a fence.

"So, what's the problem, boys?" Ruby asks, digging her hands into her sweatshirt pocket.

"Playing football," Jasper says.

"More like *not* playing football," Mo adds with a smirk.

"Jasper thinks he's too good for nine-year-old football, like he's your man Mahomes already," Mo says. "And my mom thinks I'll get hurt just *thinking* about getting tackled. What should we do?"

Ruby takes Kendall's leash from Jasper and walks toward a big oak tree, thinking hard.

"I've got it!" she says. "Did you see Coach Sanders's flyer in the community center? He's holding tryouts for a nine-and-under flag football team. The tryouts are in the park after school tomorrow. We should all give it a shot."

"Hold on," Jasper replies. "I've got way too much talent for *flag* football."

"Jasper, are you sure about that?" Ruby replies. "You might want to play on a real team before you put yourself in the Hall of Fame."

Mo nods his head in agreement.

"And, Mo, flag football is super safe," Ruby adds. "There's no tackling. You just yank on a flag. Your mom will love it."

But Jasper and Mo are not convinced.

"Look," Ruby says. "I can pull up the rules on my phone."

FLAG FOOTBALL

In flag football, physical contact between players is not allowed, which means no tackling or blocking like in tackle football. Instead, players wear two flags that hang off their belt. To "tackle" the ballcarrier, a defender must pull off one of their flags.

TACKLE

*RULES**

- The starting team has four downs to cross midfield. Upon reaching midfield, the team has three more downs to score a touchdown. A "down" is simply another way to say a "chance," "turn," or "attempt."

FORWARD PASS

- All passes must be thrown forward and caught beyond the line of scrimmage.

*Based on the official NFL FLAG rules available at nflflag.com.

- The quarterback has seven seconds to get rid of the ball.
- Offensive players must steer clear of the rusher and may not get in their way.
- Any defensive player lined up seven yards off the line of scrimmage is eligible to rush.
- If the defense intercepts a pass, then the ball remains live and they can advance it until being tackled, stepping out of bounds, or scoring.
- The ball is dead when any of the following happens:
    - The ball hits the ground.
    - The offensive player's flag is pulled from their belt.
    - The ballcarrier steps out of bounds.
    - The ballcarrier's body—other than their hands or feet—touches the ground.

OUT OF BOUNDS

"Flag football is too easy," whines Jasper.

"And I'm sure my mom will still find *something* to worry about," adds Mo. "She worries so much, she's convinced that my stuffed animals are lonely because I don't play with them anymore."

Ruby throws up her arms in frustration.

"You two are too much!" she yells. "Let's at least try out for the team. If we don't like it, we walk away. No pressure. Deal?"

Jasper looks at Mo. Mo whispers to Jasper. "Deal!" they both yell.

CHAPTER 4

SLINGING THE PIGSKIN

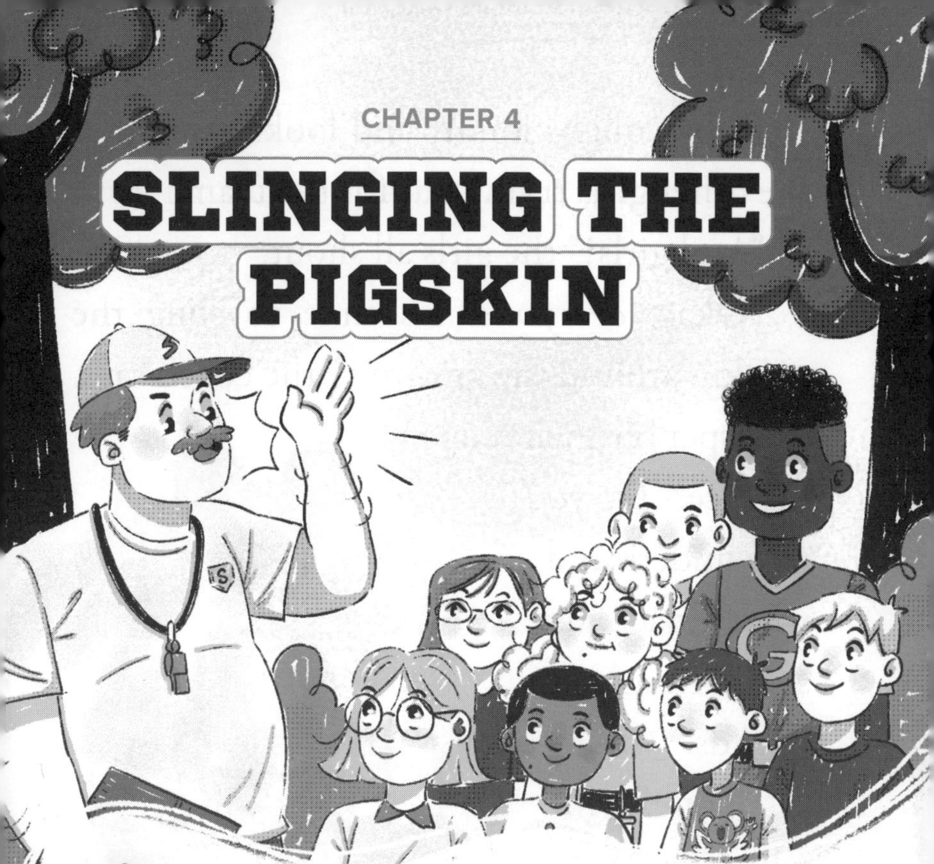

Coach Sanders stands in the middle of the Raintree Park field just as team tryouts are about to begin. He has the tall, chubby look of a former football player. A shiny silver whistle dangles from his neck, and he holds a clipboard to his side.

"Snap to it, boys!" he yells.

Ruby coughs loudly and looks around at the other girls trying out for the team.

"And girls!" the girls all shout.

"Okay, *everyone*. It's time to sling the pigskin around the gridiron," the coach says.

Jasper scrunches up his face. "Do you two understand what Coach just said?" he asks his friends.

"Nope," Mo whispers. "What language is that?!"

"When Coach says 'pigskin,' he's talking about the ball," Ruby says. "Footballs used to be made from pigs. And the 'gridiron' is the playing field. A long time ago, football fields were marked up in a checkerboard pattern like a grid."

Coach Sanders picks up a football and walks toward the end zone. "Follow me," he tells the kids.

PARTS OF A FOOTBALL FIELD

In the NFL, the field is one hundred yards long, while the end zones are another ten yards deep. When a team advances the ball into the end zone, they score a touchdown. Yard lines are spaced five yards apart all the way down both sides of the field. Hash marks are spaced one yard apart between the yard lines. Sidelines mark the edges of the field. If a player steps on the sideline, they are considered out of bounds.

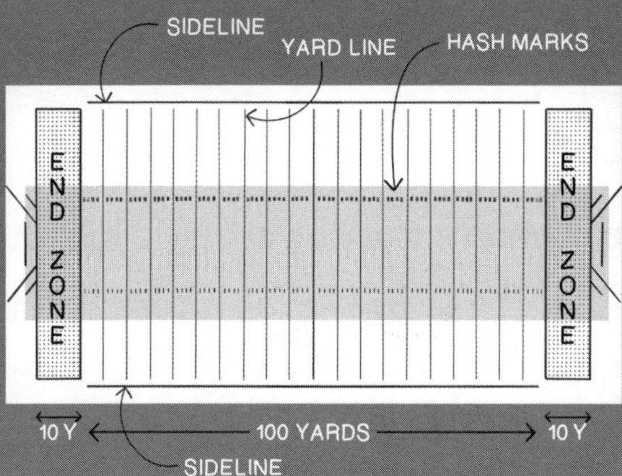

"This is where I made history." Coach Sanders has a tear in his eye and a lump in his throat as he recalls his brief moment of glory when he was sixteen years old. "I was the backup quarterback on the Raintree High Junior Varsity football team," he says, beaming. "I recovered a fumble in this very same end zone for the game-tying touchdown."

The moment was the athletic highlight of Coach Sanders's life (even though Raintree ended up losing that game in overtime to the worst team in the league). And he never lets anyone forget it.

None of the kids cares one bit.

"Can we start the tryouts now?" Jasper sighs.

"Oh, right! Let's practice some offense," Coach Sanders says, snapping back to reality. He sends half the kids to the left hash mark, the other half—including Jasper, Mo, and Ruby—to the right.

"Kids on the right side, you run ten-yard buttonhooks. Kids on the left, you run slants over the middle," he orders. "I'll be QB, just like old times when I was the best second-string JV quarterback this town has ever seen. I'll start on the right!"

Jasper is first in line on the right side, ready to impress the other kids with his slick moves.

Coach Sanders yells, "Hike!"

Jasper takes off running. He can already hear his announcer voice: *Jasper McCoy was a star in the living room and now look at him! This is the most amazing tryout I've ever seen in my life!*

CHAPTER 5

BUTTONHOOKS AND BELLY BUTTONS

Jasper feels a burning sensation in his chest as it dawns on him that he has no idea what Coach Sanders has asked him to do.

So he just keeps running straight ahead. After about fifteen steps—

Wham! The football bounces off his back.

"Looks like the ol' cannon still has some juice!" Coach Sanders says proudly. "But don't you know what a buttonhook is, young man?"

Jasper rubs his back. "Not really, but I'm pretty sure that wasn't it," he replies.

"Run straight ahead for ten yards, then turn around quick. And catch the ball with your hands, not your back!" says the coach.

Some kids laugh, pretending to get hit in the back.

"Cut it out," says Mo, standing up for his friend.

"Yeah, like any of you know the difference between a buttonhook and a belly button," Ruby adds.

Jasper is thankful for his friends' support. Still, this is not how he thought his tryout would go. He walks to the end of the line, dragging his feet. He can hear his announcer voice: *Geez, Jasper made a big mistake. He sure doesn't belong on this field!*

Now it is time for the first kid on the left hash mark to catch a pass.

"Well, look who's trying out. It's Nick Wolf," Mo says to Ruby. "The best athlete in all of Raintree."

"Hike!" the coach yells.

Hike!
WHOOSH!

Ruby is next up on the right side of the field. She is determined to run a perfect pass pattern.

“Hike!” Coach Sanders yells again.

Hike!
WHOOSH!

Touchdown!
Woo-hoo! It doesn't get any better than that, kiddos!

After all the kids have had a chance to catch a pass, it's time to practice defense.

"Okay, let's see who can pull a flag!" Coach Sanders yells. "Who wants to give it a try?"

Jasper loves defense. He always sacked his dad in the living room. But for the first time, it occurs to him that maybe his father *let* him tackle him. And he's never pulled a flag off anybody. Not even once.

But Mo is ready for the challenge. "I'll do it, Coach!" he yells.

"Great, thank you for stepping up, Mo," Coach Sanders says. "I need my best receiver to catch a pass. Nick Wolf, get over here!"

Nick lines up across from Mo. Mo stares hard at Nick, hoping to intimidate his rival. Nick laughs before running down the field. Coach Sanders throws him the ball. Nick catches it and jumps to his right, then fakes to his left. He runs all the way into the end zone, spiking the ball in celebration.

"Touchdown!" Nick yells before howling like a wolf.

"Not so fast, my friend!" Ruby yells back, pointing at Mo.

Mo has a big grin on his face. And in his right hand, much to Nick's surprise, he holds a red flag.

Coach Sanders yells, "Tackled him for just a short gain! Didn't you hear the whistle, Nicky? Great defense, Mo-Mo!"

"Nice work, Mo," Jasper says softly before his announcer voice takes over. *Ruby and Mo have stepped up with big plays in today's tryout, football fans! But Jasper? I'm not sure he's done enough to make the team.*

CHAPTER 6

HIGH HOPES

Coach Sanders gathers all the players at midfield. The tryout is over. Twenty-one kids showed up, but only twelve will make the cut.

"Everybody played well," the coach says. "Most of you will make the team. For those who don't, I know you'll feel lower than a cricket lying on his belly. But life's not all cookies and lollipops. I'll email your parents in the morning with the final roster."

Nick Wolf cheers and high-fives Dougie Jefferson, a tall boy in a Green Bay Packers jersey. They're sure they will make the team.

Mo picks up his water bottle and takes a nervous gulp.

Jasper lifts his T-shirt over his head and walks slowly toward the sidewalk. Underneath his shirt, he is crying. He is certain all the coach will remember about him is the ball that bonked off his back. "I never should have tried out," he mutters.

Just as Jasper pulls his shirt back down, a blur whizzes by him.

Mo has tripped on his own shoelaces. "Ow!" he shouts.

Jasper reaches out his hand, pulling his friend up from the ground. "It's okay, Mo," he says. "I'm nervous, too. I was a hero in my living room but a zero out on the field."

"How about a little confidence, boys?!" Ruby says to her friends. "You both did great. I feel good about our chances to make the team. We've *got* this."

Ruby holds out a stiff-arm, just like the Heisman Trophy pose.

HEISMAN TROPHY

The Heisman Trophy has been presented annually since 1935 to the nation's top college football player. It is considered one of the most famous awards in all of sports. Winners receive a 45-pound statue of a ballcarrier giving a stiff-arm.

Ruby's words make Jasper and Mo feel a little better. But all they can do now is wait for Coach Sanders's decision in the morning.

"Just relax," Ruby says as they walk home. "Maya Angelou said something like: 'Hope for the best, prepare for the worst, and don't be surprised by anything in between.'"

"What team did Maya play for?" asks Jasper.

"She didn't play football, silly. She was a famous writer!" Ruby laughs.

"Well, I'm with Maya," Mo says. "I *hope* we all make the team."

Jasper keeps walking toward his house, his announcer voice kicking in. *Jasper should be with Maya, too: prepared for the worst. Is there any possible way he will make this team?*

Tomorrow Jasper will find out. But tonight, he won't sleep a wink.

CHAPTER 7

YOU'VE GOT MAIL

Most mornings, Jasper wakes up the fourth time his mom screams "TIME TO WAKE UP, JAAASSSSPERRR!" But today, Jasper awakens before sunrise.

He jumps on his parents' bed. "CHECK YOUR EMAILS, PLEASE!" he yells.

Jasper's dad is fast asleep, snoring loudly. He sounds like a space alien.

His mom sits up, rubbing her eyes. "Who, what . . . why are you up so early, Jasper?"

"How can you sleep at a time like this?!" he replies. "I need to know if I made the team!"

Jasper's mom plops her head back down on her pillow. "It's 4:59 a.m., Jasper. Go back to bed and we'll check at breakfast."

There's no way he can sleep. Jasper walks downstairs and leaves a note on the table to let his parents know where he's going.

He slips out the door in his pajamas, walking down the block to Ruby's house.

He finds a tennis ball on the ground and tosses it at Ruby's window. *Thud. Thud.*

Finally, Ruby pokes her head out, and Jasper motions for her to come outside.

"What are you doing, Jasper?" she asks.

"Two words," Jasper replies. "Flag football. And four more words: Did we make it?"

"Oh, right! Mo's mom and dad always wake up early," Ruby says. "Let's go find out!"

Over at Mo's house, Mo and his parents are eating breakfast in the kitchen when Jasper and Ruby barge through the back door.

"Hello, you two!" Mo's mom says.

"Great timing! We were just about to read the email from Coach Sanders," says Mo's dad. "Here's wishing you all good luck!"

Mo's mom clicks on the email.

FROM: Coach Sanders

Dear Families,

If you're reading this, it means your kiddo has fire in their belly. In football, it's all about the Jimmys and Joes, not the X's and O's. And your Jimmy or Joe (or Jenny or Flo) has what it takes!

JIMMYS AND JOES, NOT X'S AND O'S

When football coaches refer to "Jimmys and Joes, not X's and O's," they mean that what matters most are the players rather than the plays that are called. That's because offensive and defensive players are depicted by X's and O's on a typical football diagram.

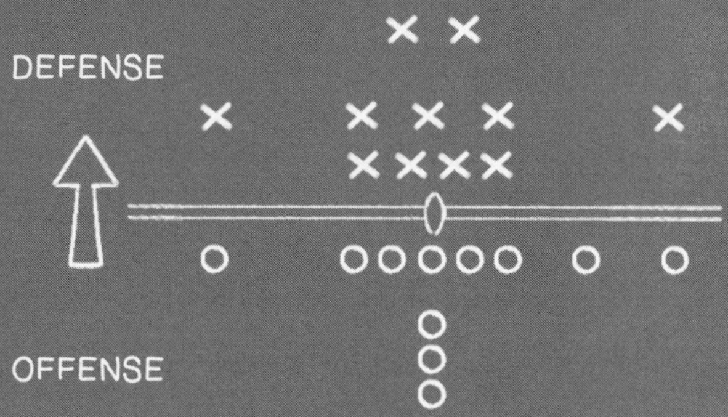

It takes Mo a second to figure out what this means. Then, it hits him: He made the team. "Yesssss!!!!" he yells. "That's what I'm talking about!!"

"What about us?" Ruby asks.

"Did we make it, too?" Jasper adds.

"Hmmm," says Mo's mom. "Let me check to see if Coach emailed your parents, too. Yamamoto . . . Berry . . ."

"Mom! Did they make it?" Mo pleads.

"McCoy . . . Jones! Yes, you all made it!" she says.

"Congratulations to the three of you!" adds Mr. Garcia.

Jasper, Mo, and Ruby start laughing and high-fiving one another. Jasper can hear the excitement in his announcer voice! *These good friends are officially flag football players. And their first practice is at 5 p.m. tonight!*

CHAPTER 8

MEET THE FROGS

When Coach Sanders arrives at Raintree Park for the team's first practice, he has to weave his way through what looks like an overcrowded campground just to get out on the football field: wagons, folding chairs, blankets, tents, and coolers-on-wheels.

"What is going on here?" Coach Sanders says to no one in particular. "Back in my day, parents had better things to do than watch practice . . ."

Ruby hops off her scooter, wearing a blue-and-red jersey with number 78 in big white numerals. She has the best collection of sports jerseys in town.

"Who are you wearing today?" Mo asks.

"It's the Sack Man, of course," Ruby beams. "Bruce Smith! I'm going to sack the QB like Bruce today. Just watch me!"

BRUCE SMITH

Bruce Smith was an all-American defensive lineman at Virginia Tech and the first overall pick in the 1985 NFL Draft by the Buffalo Bills. He was inducted into the Pro Football Hall of Fame in 2009 as one of the greatest pass rushers in football history. Smith sacked the quarterback two hundred times over the course of his nineteen-year career, setting an NFL record.

Jasper is startled by a cloud of smoke that wafts over from the street.

A bright red sports car screeches to a stop. Nick Wolf hops out, dressed in a purple-and-white satin sweat suit. "Hoooowwwwwwlll!" he yells. "This wolf is hungry!"

"Surprise, surprise, look who thinks he's the team captain already," Jasper says to his friends.

Coach Sanders calls everyone to midfield.

Jasper looks around to see who else made the team.

"Okay, my friends. You made it! Now it's time for an important decision," Coach Sanders says. "We need a team name. Something that will strike fear in the hearts of our opponents. Anybody have an idea?"

"The Nick Wolfs!" says Nick Wolf.

The other kids groan.

"The Speckled Bananas!" says Mo. "Those squishy ones are scary!"

Coach Sanders cannot believe what he's hearing. "Listen up, crib lizards," he says, "we need a name that's tough, like a real NFL team!"

"Oh, you mean like the super-scary Miami *Dolphins*?" says Ruby.

"Point taken," says Coach Sanders. "But still. What animal scares you the most?"

The kids shout out answers.

"Hairy spiders!" shouts Amir.

"Hippopotamuses!" adds Meg.

"Rattlesnakes!" suggests Ali.

"Poison dart frogs!" yells Dougie.

"Butterflies!" Eugene shouts.

"What? Why?" asks Mo.

"They start as caterpillars, but then grow wings and fly. That's scary," says Eugene.

Coach Sanders runs his hands through his hair. "Not exactly what I had in mind, but let's vote," he says. "Write down your favorite team name on a piece of paper and put it in my hat."

One by one, the kids place their ballots in the coach's sweaty blue baseball cap.

After counting the votes, Coach Sanders blows into his hands like a trumpet. "We have a team name!" he declares.

The parents inch closer, straining to hear.

"Listen up, everybody," he says. "It is my honor to introduce the toughest bunch of 9U flag football players this side of the Ohio River. Meet your poisonous Dart Frogs!"

CHAPTER 9

FLOSSING IS IMPORTANT

When Jasper, Mo, and Ruby arrive at the park for practice number two, they spot Coach Sanders doing deep knee bends.

"Seventy-eight, seventy-nine," he huffs. "Eighty! Takes a while to rev the ol' engine these days. Gather around, Frogs!"

The kids form a circle around their coach.

"If there's one thing I learned playing ball, it's that a team is more than just a collection of individuals," Coach Sanders says. "On a great team, it's one for all and all for one. So, let's get to know one another better. Tell us something special about you."

The kids glance around, wondering who will speak first.

"I can solve a Rubik's Cube in twenty-two seconds," says Nick.

"I can burp the national anthem," says Eugene.

"I moved here from Texas last week," says Sofia. "I've been on seventeen roller coasters."

"I'm Douglas Jefferson Jr., but you can call me Dougie," says the tallest kid on the team. "You've probably seen my dance videos online."

"What was the question?" Ella asks. "Oh, I believe in unicorns but not ghosts."

"I love to draw," says Amir, holding a piece of construction paper. "Check out this team logo I sketched last night!"

After the rest of the kids have shared fun facts about themselves, Coach Sanders hands every player a piece of paper. On the front, there are four diagrams.

THE DART FROGS' OFFENSIVE PLAYS

- Banana Sundae with Nuts

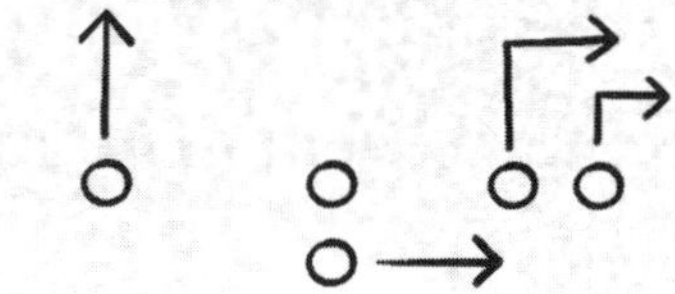

- Blueberry Flapjacks

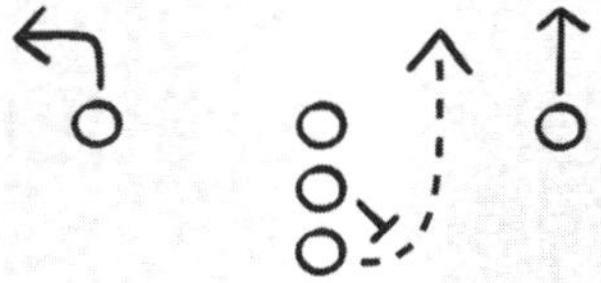

- Purple Puppy Power!

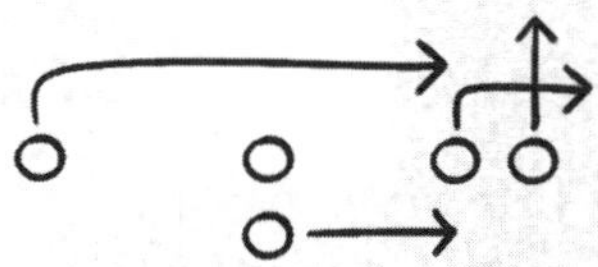

- Tennessee Tornado

Scanning the names of the offensive plays, Jasper turns to Ruby and Mo. "I don't know if these plays will get us touchdowns," he says. "But I do know we'll never forget what they're called!"

Mo motions for Jasper to shush because Coach Sanders is talking.

"It's pretty simple, Frogs," Coach says. "If you learn what's on the front of this piece of paper, we'll play good football. If you do what's on the back, we'll have a good time and your smile will show it."

Jasper turns the paper over.

"You mean floss like this?" Meg asks, swaying her hips and arms like the popular floss dance move.

"Go, Meggie! Go, Meggie!" Dougie and Eugene shout.

"No, like *this*," Coach says, pretending to floss his teeth.

"Oh," says Dougie, disappointed.

"No fun!" says Eugene.

Coach Sanders tosses a football from hand to hand. "Now, let's practice our plays. We've got a game tomorrow!"

Jasper sprints across the field, barely able to contain his excitement. One more sleep until he plays in his very first *real* football game.

CHAPTER 10

SACK ATTACK

Good morning, everybody! You're looking liiive at Raintree Park as the Dart Frogs take on the Brentwood Beagles. Today is the season opener for both teams. This game should be a real nail-biter! Jasper hears his announcer voice as he stretches before the game.

Over on the sidelines, Jasper's and Ruby's moms are leading cheers. "*F-R-O-G-S*, we're the team that is the best!"

Mo's mom no longer seems too worried about her son playing football. Instead, she's gone all-in on frog-themed gear. Draped in a green-and-gold blanket printed with pictures of frogs, she sips from a trendy frog-green water bottle. Even her cell phone case is bedazzled with sparkling mini frogs.

Jasper tightens his belt around his waist and looks over toward his dad.

"You can do this, Jasper!" his dad shouts, giving him a thumbs-up. "Just like in the living room!"

Even Kendall barks his encouragement.

Jasper puts on his most-serious game face and glares over at the Beagles.

Mo prepares for the game by sprinting up and down the field.

Ruby stands under a tree, running through the offensive plays in her mind.

Meanwhile, Nick Wolf spreads black paint under his eyes, fastens on a pair of leather receiver's gloves, and lets out one final "hooowwwwl."

It's game time! The referee whistles a start to the game.

Soon, the Frogs have used up three downs. They have one chance left to cross midfield.

FROGS' FOURTH DOWN
WHOOSH!
DART FROGS
DART FROGS

My gloves were too slippery! The ball was wet!
It's okay, Nick! We've got your back on defense!
GO FROGS
Go, Ruby!

BEAGLES' FIRST DOWN
SACK!
BEAGLES' SECOND DOWN
SACK!

BEAGLES' THIRD DOWN
DART FROGS
SACK!
Three sacks in a row!!
She didn't let the QB throw the ball even once! Way to go, Ruby!

Neither team moves the ball very far on the next two possessions. When the halftime whistle sounds, the score is still tied 0–0.

Coach Sanders calls the team together in a huddle. “Never expected we’d be sitting on goose eggs at intermission, but sometimes that’s the way the cookie crumbles,” he says.

Ruby looks at Jasper and silently mouths, “What is he talking about?”

Jasper just shakes his head and softly says, “I have no idea. But this talk about cookies is making my stomach growl.”

Jasper can hear his announcer voice over the rumbling of his stomach. *The Beagles and Dart Frogs are locked in a scoreless battle. Jasper still has a lot to prove. To score a touchdown, he has to get the ball. Can he do it? Is he hungry for victory, or just for a snack? Stay tuned!*

CHAPTER 11

BANANA SUNDAE

Finishing his halftime remarks, Coach Sanders fires up his team with one last command: "Let's show 'em how the big dogs hunt in the second half!"

"Wait, we are the Frogs, not the Beagles. And aren't beagles *small* dogs?" Meg asks Ali.

"Just go with it," Ali replies. "He thinks he's inspiring us."

Jasper knows that if the Dart Frogs are going to win this game, they need points. When he played living-room football, he scored touchdowns almost every time.

So, he gets up the nerve to suggest a play. "Coach, I've been thinking. I know a play that will get us a touchdown," he says.

Coach Sanders smiles. "Good thinking, McCoy," he says.

Jasper imagines scoring a touchdown on Steamboat Springs, his favorite play that his dad dreamed up. He knows Coach Sanders will love it. "Let's run—"

But Coach Sanders interrupts Jasper before he can even get "Steamboat" out of his mouth. The coach has already turned to the players on the field, telling them, "Let's run Banana Sundae with Nuts for Nick."

Jasper watches from the sidelines as the other Frogs line up in formation: two receivers are split to the right and Nick stands all alone on the left.

Not only did Coach Sanders not wait to hear Jasper's suggestion, he didn't even put him in the game.

Mo lines up a few yards behind the center, catches the snap, fakes a handoff to Ali, and sprints toward the sideline.

All the Beagles think Mo is going to throw a short pass. But just as he approaches the line of scrimmage, he stops and gathers his feet. Then he throws a rainbow across the field to Nick.

HOW TO THROW A SPIRAL

Grip the ball with your fingertips on the laces. Hold it slightly toward the back of the ball.

Extend your arm forward and flick your wrist downward as you let go of the ball.

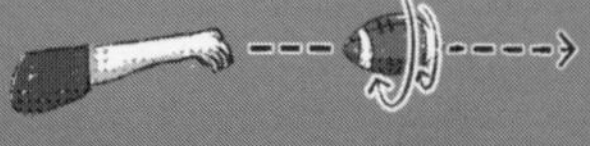

The ball takes so long to arc its way toward Nick, he has time to wave at the Beagles defenders before he even catches the pass.

And once Nick does, he races down the field with his flags blowing in the breeze and not a Beagle in sight.

Touchdown, Dart Frogs!

The other Frogs hug Nick and jump around, howling. But Jasper stays seated on the bench. The truth is that even though his team is now winning the game, Jasper isn't happy. He was frustrated that Coach Sanders called a play for Nick and jealous when Nick scored. Not to mention all Nick's howling just makes him feel worse.

Jasper goes over to Ruby. "Am I ever going to make a play?" he whispers to his friend.

CHAPTER 12

BARKING BEAGLES

"Snap out of it, Jasper!" Davey shouts as the Frogs run onto the field for defense.

"And no moping around!" adds Ruby. "We're going to need you before this game is over."

Jasper takes his position on defense, reminding himself to focus hard.

The Beagles have the ball and are easily gaining big yards.

Every time the other team makes a good play, Jasper's announcer voice describes the disaster in the making. *It looks like the Beagles are going to tie up this game. And Jasper McCoy has been a huge embarrassment—he has done absolutely nothing!*

"Jassspperrr, heads up!"

A long pass comes whistling over Jasper's head. Ruby screams for him to jump and intercept it.

But a Beagle catches the ball and scampers in for a touchdown.

Rather than tie the game, the Beagles go for a two-point conversion—and they make it.

TWO-POINT CONVERSION

A touchdown is worth six points. After scoring a touchdown in flag football, the scoring team has two options to earn additional points. They can run or pass the ball from the five-yard line for one point. Or they can run or pass it from the ten-yard line for two points. The ball must cross into the end zone on one play.

Now the Beagles are winning, 8–7. All their players are barking, and their parents are barking back.

There is time for one last drive for the Dart Frogs.

Mo grabs Jasper by the arm. "Yo, Jazz. If we score, we win. If we don't, we lose. It's as simple as that."

Jasper nods his head in agreement. *It's time for Jasper McCoy to step up. It. Is. Time,* his announcer voice says.

Just two plays later, the Frogs pass the midfield line.

Coach Sanders calls time-out. The team huddles around him. "There is time for one final play," he says. "Frogs never quit! We have to score!"

CHAPTER 13

GOBOYGO!

Coach Sanders stares at his clipboard with the team's four offensive plays written on it. Finally, he settles on another play for Nick Wolf: Purple Puppy Power! And he moves Ruby to quarterback.

Ruby looks across at the defense, calmly picturing the play in her head. "Hut, hut, hike!" she yells.

Ruby catches the snap and drops back to pass. She looks to the left to confuse the defenders, then wheels to her right.

Nick is sprinting across the field fifteen yards in front of her—exactly where he is supposed to be.

Meanwhile, Jasper follows close behind. If he isn't going to catch the ball, he at least wants to be close to the action so it looks like he did *something* in the game.

Ruby steps forward and spirals the ball toward Nick with all her might.

WHOOSH!

OHMYGOSH!
OHMYGOSH!
GOJASPER
GOOOOOOOOOOO!
GOBOYGOBOY
GOBOYGO!!!

Jasper hears the announcer voice in his head, louder than ever. *Can Jasper McCoy win this game for the Dart Frogs?!*

CHAPTER 14

TILL NEXT TIME

Jasper crosses the goal line with the game-winning touchdown!

Ruby runs over and gives Jasper a high five. “What did I tell you?” she says. “I knew we’d need you today!”

Jasper’s teammates surround him, cheering.

“Touchdown!” Mo cheers.

“We win!” Dougie shouts.

“Yes!” Meg yells, hugging her teammates.

“Great job, J-Mac!” Coach Sanders tells Jasper. “You ran faster than a rocket-powered roadrunner!”

Nick Wolf runs over, too, and gives Jasper a fist bump. “Jasper, that was an amazing catch to win the game!” he shouts. “But let’s not forget the other star of the day . . . ”

Jasper groans. He knows what is coming next. Surely, Nick will howl and tell everyone how great he is.

"Ruby!" Nick says, surprising everyone. "Her three sacks were huge and she threw the game-winning pass. Great job, Rubester!"

Coach Sanders stands tall in the middle of his players, proud of the victory. But he isn't satisfied. "We made some mistakes, but nothing we can't fix if we keep working hard," he says.

"That reminds me of something Nikki Giovanni once said," Ruby declares.

"Did she play linebacker for the Titans?" Mo asks.

"No woman has played in the NFL . . . yet," Ruby replies. "Nikki's a famous poet. And she said that she didn't mind failing, but couldn't forgive herself if she didn't try her best. So, let's keep working and get even better!"

"Keep on grinding!" the coach adds.

Jasper's mom comes up to the kids with a bag of oranges.

"Hey, Jasper," she says. "Aren't you glad I told you to quit playing football in the house?"

"You wouldn't have scored that game-winning touchdown otherwise!" Jasper's dad adds, holding Kendall by his leash.

"Facts!" Ruby says, laughing.

Jasper smiles, grabs Kendall's leash, and heads home—with Ruby on one side and Mo on the other.

The three friends can hear the sound of football games their neighbors are watching on TV. But by now, their minds are off football and on to other things.

Jasper has math homework to finish. Mo needs to practice his piano performance for the talent show. And Ruby is excited to read a book on space travel. Playing sports is fun, but it isn't *all* that matters.

"Till next time," Jasper says as he reaches his house.

"Till game time!" Mo and Ruby shout back.

ABOUT THE CREATORS

ANDREW MARANISS

lives with his family in Nashville, Tennessee. He grew up playing touch football on Sundays underneath the Washington Monument. Now he cheers on the Green Bay Packers and Vanderbilt Commodores. Andrew is a bestselling author of sports nonfiction, including the series Beyond the Game: Athletes Change the World. Sports Zone! is his first fiction series!

AISHWARYA TANDON

is an illustrator and cartoonist living in India with her family. When not working, you can find her drawing in her sketchbook, watching soccer, and daydreaming about having a pet dog like Kendall. Aishwarya illustrated the picture book *Diwali in My New Home*. Sports Zone! is her first early chapter book series!

QUESTIONS & ACTIVITIES

1. Reread page 14. Then research Patrick Mahomes. Find three more facts about him!

2. In Chapter 6, how does Jasper feel after the flag football tryouts? Have you ever felt this way? Was there something you hoped to do that didn't go as planned?

3. On page 58, Amir shares his drawing of the Dart Frogs' team logo. Name your own sports team. Then draw your team logo!

4. Reread pages 87–88. Explain why Nick calls Ruby the other star of the day.

5. Look at the comic panels across pages 84–85. Write what happens! Start with Jasper's dad cheering for him. Then describe the game action that follows!